To my parents,

Ticha Ignatius Neba

and

Ticha Esther Ufie

Table of Contents

❖ Acknowledgements...6

❖ Foreword...8

❖ Introduction...10

CHAPTER ONE...13

A PRINCIPLE-BASED LIFE

➤ God's Word Is The Standard For Determining A Man's Worth........................14

➤ Your Ability To Maintain Consistent Standards.....................................15

➤ Why Do People Follow You?...16

➤ What Is Your Value?..17

➤ Your Integrity To Your Word..18

CHAPTER TWO...21

THE RIGHT TO AND POWER OF DECISION-MAKING

➤ Allow God To Choose Through You..21

➤ Right Decisions And Incoming Storms..23

➤ Assessing Your Level Of Assurance In God's Decisions..............................25

➤ Consider God's Word To Be "Yes and Amen"...25

➤ Get Rid Of Every Escapist Mentality...26

CHAPTER THREE...29

THE POWER TO TAKE ON RESPONSIBILITIES

➤ The Importance Of Taking On Responsibilities 29

➤ Preparation For Responsibilities..30

➤ A Word To Teachers..31

CHAPTER FOUR..33

ZERO TOLERANCE

➤ Never Be Discouraged 35

CHAPTER FIVE..38

BUILDING UP A LEADERSHIP SPIRIT

➤ Defining A "Leadership Spirit"..38

➤ Know Your Limits As You Promote The Strengths Of Others...........................39

➤ How To Cultivate A Leadership Spirit..40

CHAPTER SIX..44

THE POWER OF STAYING FOCUSED

➢ Understand Who You Are...44

➢ Understand The Seasons Of Your Life...45

➢ Identify What You Need To Do 45

➢ Know How To Manage Your Desires..46

➢ Know Where And How To Get Your Goals Met 46

➢ Be Ready To Dedicate Yourself Entirely To Achieving Your Goals............47

➢ The End Result Is Worth The Investment..48

➢ See Your Life's Fulfilment Being Tied to the Realization of Your Goals......48

➢ Surround Yourself With The Right People..48

➢ Feed Your Passion...50

➢ The Glory Of Small Beginnings..51

CHAPTER SEVEN...53

TAKING YOUR AUTHORITY

➢ The Place Of Authority...53

➢ Understanding How Authority Functions..53

➢ Know Your Jurisdiction 54

➢ Be Loyal To The Authority Over You...55

➢ Give Instructions And Stick To Them—Not Opinions Or Suggestions..........55

➢ Be Fully Convicted Of The Feasibility Of Your Decision..........................56

➢ Have The Courage To Stand By Your Convictions................................... 56

➢ You Are The Leader! Never Create The Impression That "We" Are Leading.....56

➢ Prove To The People That You Have Their Best Interest At Heart 57

CHAPTER EIGHT...59

THE LEADER'S REFLEX ACTION

➢ The Implications Of Leadership...59

➢ The Reflex..59

➢ Get Rid Of The Dogmatic Mindset...61

ABOUT THE AUTHOR...64

Acknowledgements

$\mathcal{I}$ sincerely acknowledge all those who have played active roles in my Christian journey:

- ❖ Ambe Lucas, the precious minister who led me to the Lord and fathered me in my early beginnings.
- ❖ Limen William Pani, my spiritual father and mentor, a man with an uncommon spirit of excellence.
- ❖ Riccardo Meusel, who strategically and financially supported my evangelistic endeavors.
- ❖ Roy Davis, who graciously wrote the foreword to this book.
- ❖ And all those who took time off their busy schedules to proofread this book.

Foreword

I would like to express how honored I am to have been asked by my beloved co-labourer in the same vineyard to write this foreword. I believe it will prove to be an eternal beacon for church leaders and all aspiring leaders of the Body of Christ worldwide. Finally the Lord has raised up a penman who has been given insight on Kingdom principles of leadership. I assure you that if these leadership principles are read and meditated upon with patience, discernment, and understanding, all those who read it will manifest as "Sent Leaders'' of Jehovah himself. There are no stones left untouched. There are no grey areas which have not been rectified! What has been given to each willing reader of this book uniquely and without respect of position, person, or authority is revelation knowledge. Such knowledge is not readily available from the pulpit or in everyday conversations.

This book provides useful insights into true leadership abilities for all who have been summoned into to a "God-called leadership position", as well as for those who are still to be called. It provides clearly laid out principles for all to understand, as well as practical application that can be applied to one's life and calling! I must admit that I have read many books on godly leadership and attended many a seminar on pastoral leadership, but this masterpiece is unlike any other due to its uniqueness, simplicity, profoundness, and revelatory nature—all of which each of you will receive as you read this book.

If you are a pastor, deacon, elder, father, business worker or owner, professor, policewoman, judge or attorney, this is a must read for you. I highly recommend this fine penmanship of Dr. Willibroad. I cannot wait for the next "Best Seller" to be published!

Pastor Roy Pascal Davis

Senior Pastor of Church of the Nations
Founder of Shepherd's Heart World OutReach Mission Ministry
Lubbock, Texas-USA.

Introduction

$\mathcal{I}$ must confess that before the Lord finally impressed upon my spirit to write this book, He had seriously been dealing with me on the issue of leadership. I had to come to a place where I did not give any room for my youthfulness to be despised. His Word says, "Let no man despise thy youth…(1 Timothy 4:12)." To live this way is a conscious act and manner of life. It is essential to have full confidence and assurance in all that the Lord has invested in you.

You will discover that it is highly impossible to develop or cultivate a leadership spirit if you have an inferiority complex or low self-esteem. It is even more difficult to develop a leadership spirit if you question God's opinion about you or are not courageous enough to face the challenges of life.

The time has come to start nurturing the hero and champion in you. If not, you will be easily intimidated by life's challenges and live contrary to what the scripture says in Proverbs 28:1: "…but the righteous are bold as a lion." That is who we really are! I encourage you to not just read this book, but prayerfully mix your reading with faith and practice living according to all its guidelines. Only then will the secret truths in this book have the ability to awaken the giant within you.

As you start cultivating a leadership spirit within you, it should be noted that you may be misinterpreted as proud or seeking to be famous. It could also be interpreted as arrogance. Do not be discouraged or fret because this is not who you are…. absolutely not! Instead, be motivated and charged the more, for that will eventually make you become a true leader—one who will be able to command followers and be a voice of reason and refuge to those you lead.

For a long time, the Body of Christ has not been able to understand these revelational truths. They have undoubtedly given authority and power to politicians, the rich, etc. We've been living in fear and banditry all because of ignorance. When one looks at the men of old, the prophets were the advisors to kings. However, in this day and age, men of God have become silent. God never intended for the church to be second class in the society, for His Word says that "we will be the head and not the tail (Deuteronomy 28:13)." How many pastors can confront government officials, and directly tell them, "Thus saith the Lord…" without panicking?

Jim Eliot, one of the missionaries killed by the Waodani (Auca) Indians in 1956, was a student in Wheaton College in Wheaton, IL. At the age of 21, he became conscious of the direct and personal implications of the Lord Jesus' command to go and preach the Gospel and he wrote this letter to his parents:

We are so utterly ordinary, so commonplace, while we profess to know a power the 20th century does not reckon with. But we are harmless and therefore unharmed. We are spiritual pacifists, non-militants, conscientious objectors in this battle to the death with principalities and powers in high places… We are 'sideliners'—coaching and criticizing the real wrestlers while contented to sit by and leave the enemies of God unchallenged. The world cannot hate us—we are too much like its own. Oh that God would make us dangerous! (Elliot)

Dearly beloved, when the church would mature in leadership according to the cry of this young man, then leadership within nations would be influenced greatly by Church leaders. This book is essential and a must read for every Christian leader and all those who want to become champions in this present world. The Bible says: "I have said, ye are gods; and all of you are children of the Most High." But ye shall die like (mere) men…" (Psalm 82:6-7). Beloved, let us live as gods rather than to die as mere men. This scripture insinuates that we are not mere men nor common class citizens. Hence, we will not act as such.

As you embark on this journey of *Cultivating the Spirit of Leadership*, I pray today by the grace and mercy of our Lord that your life will be forever transformed. As you begin the enforcement of the divine standards for a successful and progressive impact in ministry, the giant that has been asleep within you will surely be awakened. Within these chapters you will gain valuable insights, unbeatable courage, tenacity, commitment and wisdom to sail along in life as a successful leader.

May this book be to you all that it has been to me, and all that God intends it to be to you. God bless you.

Yours in His service,

Dr. Willibroad W. Ticha

President and Founder
Gospel Heroes World Missions

Chapter One

A PRINCIPLE – BASED LIFE

One of the greatest ways of living a responsible and successful life is by living according to established principles and values. According to Galatians 5:1, we have been called out of the law into a life of freedom in Christ. But that does not imply that there will be no strict and explicit principles by which we should live. Anybody who lives a life without certain governing principles is not a mature person. This is often characteristic of an individual who has no vision, goal, or expectations of the future.

Every divine expectation of excellence and a more productive life comes with many challenges—so much so that it will only be an individual who has certain principles that will succeed. Established and deeply engrained principles will keep you longer and stronger in the battle and your victory will be inevitable. King Solomon is one of those who had experienced quite a lot in life. He was inspired by the Lord to write the book of Proverbs. In Proverbs 4:20, he instructs Christians to attend to God's words and incline their ear unto God's sayings. People who have been through a lot in life glean principles from their experiences—and their experiences can be an eye-opener to the younger generations. Furthermore, Proverbs 4:1 states "Hear, ye children, the instruction of a father, and attend to know understanding.*" It is time for the children of God to heed to His word. The time has come to establish principles and live a principle-based life. This is the lifestyle that will catapult us into maturity. Grounded principles differentiate the men from the boys. A leader once said that "an individual who lives by principle has 90% of his decisions already made". Without specific principles governing your life, you will soon become a casualty of undesired circumstances.

The reason why many people fail in the pursuit of their life goals and dreams is because of a lack of a principle-directed life. I overheard someone say this about the late Michael Jackson

(1958–2009), the legend of pop music: "He practices about a hundred times before stepping on stage for a single performance." This commitment to his gift was no doubt what gave rise to the excellence he demonstrated in the field of music. This in turn made him one of the richest and most outstanding musicians of his time. There is indeed no outstanding excellence and victory in life for an individual who lives without principles.

All the great heroes history has ever known were people of particular principles. No matter how hard it was to abide by these principles, these individuals would not give up. As a church and as individuals, we really need to start living by specific and stringent principles regarding our goals in life and ministry. This is one of those very important factors that must first be put in place if we will succeed to cultivate a leadership spirit—for without a principle-oriented life, an individual becomes cheap and despised in the eyes of men.

God's Word Is The Standard For Determining A Man's Worth

It is imperative that we pay close attention to this very crucial point as the standards and integrity of God's word are at stake. For a better comprehension of this point, it will be advisable to closely study the scriptures below:

My brethren, have not the faith of our Lord Jesus Christ, the Lord of glory, with respect of persons. For if they come unto your assembly a man with a gold ring, in goodly apparels, and there come in also a poor man in vile raiment; And ye have respect to him that weareth the gay clothing, and say unto him, sit thou here in a good place, and say to the poor, stand thou there, or sit here under my footstool; Are ye not then partial in yourselves, and are become judges of evil thoughts?" (James 2:1-4).

What is evident in the above text is that there are a series of things which are quite crucial when it comes to the faith and also in cultivating a leadership spirit. James 1:1 states, "James, a bondservant of God and of the Lord Jesus Christ, to the twelve tribes who are in the Dispersion: Greetings." We notice from the above scripture that the whole epistle of James was not only addressed to a particular group of people in Israel (like some of the other epistles) but to all of the twelve tribes of Israel scattered everywhere. This gives clear indication about the importance of this book.

James admonished these tribes not to have the faith of our Lord Jesus with respect of persons. We can conclude from James' statement that there would be situations where a minister of the Gospel would be tempted to compromise certain virtues and standards of the Word in order to somehow favor an individual or group of persons. As ministers, we must be very careful not to give priority to individuals in such a way that we end up compromising the Word. In fact, a minister who has no respect of persons but is willing to preach the uncompromising Word is the minister who would be used most by God.

This firm decision by a minister to give God's Word preference—regardless of persons—is key to cultivating this kind of leadership (champion-like authoritative) spirit. This kind of minister will never feel threatened or intimidated by the presence of any individual, irrespective of his achievements, position in society, etc. The Word of God through such a minister has now become a 'voice' and not a 'noise'. We need to embrace this truth as one of our governing principles as we relate with all manner of people; great and small. Have no regard for an individual's 'gold ring' (i.e. authority, kingship) not even his 'apparel' (i.e. affluence, wealth), but only the Word of God. That alone will cause everyone who comes into contact with you to recognize and respect your position and authority as a servant of God. That is when the anointing on your head (life) will be able to flow down to be a blessing to them as recorded in Psalm 133 below:

> Behold, how good and pleasant it is for brothers to dwell together in unity! It is like the precious ointment on the head that ran down on the beard, even Aaron's (the priest or minister) beard that went down to the shirts of his garments. It is as the dew of Hermon and as the dew that descended on the mountains of Zion, for there the LORD commanded the blessing, even life forever.

When cultivating a leadership spirit, there will be greater loyalty among those led and a perception that they need you more than you really need them. This cannot be accomplished through speech but through action. Never give your people the impression that they are there to meet your financial needs. They would soon avoid you which would result in you losing their loyalty and esteem. Focus on being a blessing to them spiritually and in any other way you can. This will result in a flock who will rally around you, support you and whose devotion you will not lose.

Let us follow Jesus' example as He prayed to the Father in John 17:12. He stated that of all those that the Father gave Him, He had lost none (except the son of perdition). This was because Jesus was everything to the twelve disciples, both spiritually and otherwise. I am reminded of an instance when some of His followers left Him because they refused to accept His teachings. When this happened, He asked the twelve whether they will leave as well too. But Peter and the rest responded: "...Lord, to whom shall we go? Thou hast the words of eternal life" (John 6:68). What indeed kept them bound to Jesus was the fact that He had something that they could identify with as divine and trustworthy and which could lead to their development and fulfilment. He was the immediate miracle to every lack they ever experienced.

Your Ability To Maintain Consistent Standards

The Bible warns us against prejudice in James 2:1-4. In these verses, we learn that one

15

very important virtue to develop if we want to be able to cultivate a leadership spirit is the ability to maintain the same standards as we interact with people. These standards should be maintained regardless of the person's economic or social status. Leaders must avoid portraying any form of partiality or discrimination. This is a vital and sensitive point when it comes to cultivating a leadership spirit. We must be able to interact with people from all walks of life. We must deal with different personalities, irrespective of their various positions in society with the same degree of love, concern and respect - This is what differentiates true and godly leadership from secular leadership where there could be displays of favouritism and discrimination.

An effective leader has outgrown a stereotyped mentality and possess a more flexible type of mentality. Having a flexible mentality however does not alter the standards of operation or the virtues of life. In this way, you will stand strong both in adversities, in storms, and when it feels like everything else is falling apart. Remember Ephesians 6:13 which says: "Wherefore... having done all, to stand." This is where the challenge lies. Once this leadership spirit is cultivated, then the resolve to remain standing becomes obvious. One thing about leadership is that followers are able to point out a bad leader without any thought – and they would be correct 90% of the time. This does not mean that being a good leader necessarily means pleasing people- far from it. On the other hand, there are scenarios where real and genuine leaders are also resented by the people. To be a good leader requires truthfulness and integrity to your assignments and duties, while endeavouring to maintain the love and respect of those who follow you.

Why Do People Follow You?

One of the greatest discoveries a leader can make is to find out why a person or group of people submit to or follow his leadership. Instead of being excited that one has a great following, it is of more importance to understand the motives of your followers. Understanding their motives will help you to determine whether you are wasting your time by investing time and potential in them or not. The scripture teaches us that it is useless "giving to a dog what is holy", or "cast pearls to a swine, else they trample them under their feet, and turn again and rend you (Matthew 7:6)". In fact, it is to this end that Proverbs. 29:1 speaks when it pronounced destruction on whosoever keeps receiving instructions and would not accept it for a change.

In John 6:26-71, Jesus is likened to the living bread that came from heaven and whoever will not eat His body and drink His blood has no life. This was a difficult truth. Jesus did not compromise His teaching so that the disciples who left Him would return. Instead, He asked the twelve if they would also leave. Peter's response was, "To whom shall we go to, Thou has the word of life?" This response pleased the heart of Jesus as He knew that the twelve had understood the real reason why they should follow Him - He has the words of eternal life. This was indeed why Jesus came into the world as seen in John 3:16 and John 17:3:

"For God so loved the world, that he gave His only begotten Son, so that whoever believes in Him, should not perish, but have everlasting life."

"And this is life eternal, that they might know You, the only true God, and Jesus Christ, whom You have sent."

Once people are not able to realize why they should be under a particular leadership, the ministry will not be able to advance as it should, neither will they discover nor fulfil their individual divine purposes. This will result in unnecessary problems, division, and at times, second guessing of the leadership. That is why as leaders we are admonished to "write down the vision, and make it plain upon tables, that he may run that readeth it (Habakkuk 2:2)." This means that a people should be under a particular leadership or ministry because they can identify and relate with the mandate of that commission. They should also be willing to passionately run with it at whatever cost. Any other reason would be wrong and selfish. An individual should not be under someone's leadership because of their popularity, the opportunity to have connections with other ministers internationally, or because they want to benefit from the leader's fortune or for any other selfish reason. If that is the case, the individual will not be able to fulfil the mandate even in the face of challenges. Should he eventually be able to gain the influence desired, he will not speak well of his former leader and may join others to criticize him. It is true that there are benefits that pertain to following a particular leader. However, one's most pertinent reason should be that one identifies with the mandate and is willing to run with the vision.

What is Your Value?

Beloved, in cultivating this leadership spirit, you must ensure that you possess something undisputable that would give you an advantage over others. This is a call for every minister of God and Christian in general to improve themselves worthy as the level of one's self-worth determines their world and sphere of influence. It is time, as a minister of God, to increase your level of self-worth. Even a fool realizes that empty vessels have no goods to deliver. This is a fundamental principle which every individual who aspires to become a voice in whatever field must ensure. The scripture says: "We should study to show ourselves approved, a workman who has no reason whatsoever to be ashamed (2 Timothy 2: 5)."

People secure their place in life based on what they can offer, for an audience is never granted to an individual who is not an embodiment of treasure. The time has come to use your talents to build up inner strength so as to increase your worth. The result would be people hunting down our addresses and desiring to be directed by our skills and competences. Once you understand your value, you will be able to define the principles you will live by. It takes only such established self-principles to conserve your value. Principles attract the public to trust your value or worth. For example, a business man who talks carelessly and disrespectfully to his clients will chase away possible clients irrespective of the product. It takes character to market your goods and services.

Your Integrity to Your Word

It is worth noting that a man's worth is usually judged by comparing his words with his corresponding actions. That is what differentiates an actor from a joker. Being able to maintain your words and act upon them accordingly determines whether you are a man who can be taken at his word. Consider this Biblical text: "LORD, who shall abide in thy tabernacle? Who shall dwell in thy holy hill? …He that sweareth to his own hurt, and changeth not (Psalm 15:1, 4)."
We realize from the text above that God indeed has an inheritance for His own. He places great value on those who have grown into maturity in Him to the extent that they understand the importance of keeping to their word without change or compromise. Listen and think before you utter words and always be careful to watch and guard what you say, knowing that you would become a debtor to every word that proceeds from your mouth. In cultivating a leadership spirit, you must listen keenly and patiently as well as develop a principle of scrutinising every thought in your heart before it becomes a spoken word. A view of the leaders of large democratic countries will prove that leaders are taken at every word they speak. Those campaigning for offices of responsibility are usually voted into office based on the ideas they project, their responses to questions, and eventually when they do take up office, they are judged by the words and promises they made during their campaign. Your words have the power to either excuse, accuse or accredit you as recorded in the scriptures below:

> Any story sounds true until someone tells the other side and sets the record straight… It is harder to win back the friendship of an offended brother than to capture a fortified city. His anger shuts you out like iron bars. Ability to give wise advice satisfies like a good meal! Those who love to talk will suffer the consequences. Men have died for saying the wrong thing! (Proverbs.18:17-21 TLB).

This would imply that words spoken have a way of accrediting a leader before the people.

Why most leaders talk unrealistically is because of their desire to lead at all costs. They want to win the approval of the people and consequently find themselves making promises which they cannot deliver. In order to preserve their reputation, leaders have to be real and true. The Bible says in Ecclesiastes 7:1 that "a good reputation is more valuable than the most expensive perfume". A leader who cannot commit himself to the words he utters cannot find people who would commit to following him or who would take him at his word. Not only that, but such a leader will lose his influence and authority over life's situations and his authority before God. For God does not make a man's words law when the man does not commit himself to whatever he utters. Note the scripture: "Thou shalt also decree a thing and it shall be established unto thee... (Job 22:28)". This can only be based on such a foundation where the scriptures have become true in the life of an individual. This is essential in cultivating a leadership spirit, for God has highly exalted His word above His name as scriptures evidently portrays: "I will worship toward Thy holy temple, and praise Thy name for Thy lovingkindness and for Thy truth: for Thou hast magnified Thy Word above all Thy Name (Psalm 138:2)." It is undeniably evident that the psalmist has full assurance in God's personality and integrity. He has always kept to His Word, to a point that warrants our worship and praise. Your level of influence is determined by your level of integrity. This implies that if He fails His Word, then, He no longer deserves to answer His Name (title). Therefore, a man's title and status is only worth his degree of commitment to the words he utters. Get committed to your words no matter how much it will demand from you, and you will soon become the voice people will hearken to.

Chapter Two

THE RIGHT TO AND POWER OF DECISION-MAKING

It is obvious that every individual has the right to make decisions since God has given us a choice: "I (the Lord) call heaven and earth to record this day against you, that I have set before you life and death, blessing and cursing: therefore choose... (Deuteronomy 30:19)." It is worth noting that our focus in this chapter is not simply to talk about the fact that we have the liberty to make decisions and actions in the various aspects of our lives. The chapter also highlights the fact that we need to examine what it takes to make the kind of decisions that would bring us to a position of significance and relevance. This will ultimately result in our victory over the challenges of life. That is really where the power of success lies.

Allow God To Choose Through You

Considering that we want to consistently make decisions which will cause us to be victorious (regardless of the surrounding storms of life), we need to allow the Lord God to choose through us. He is the embodiment of all wisdom and knowledge, and He knows the end from the beginning. This may sound absurd to the individual who is still full of himself rather than the Spirit of God. Take another look the following scripture: "I call heaven and earth to record this day against you that I have set before you life and death, blessing and cursing: therefore choose life, that both thou and thy seed may live (Deuteronomy 30:19)." It is time we examine the above verse of scripture critically in order to be able to comprehend the lesson taught by the Spirit of God. First of all, take note that He said that heaven and earth would record that day against us – the day wherein we are being given the liberty to make a choice for ourselves. The reason for the words AGAINST US is because God does not actually want us to take decisions independent of what His exact will per time and situation for us is. He has given us a will. No doubt Apostle Paul said in

Acts 20:26-27 (TLB): "Let me say this plainly that no man's blood can be laid at my door, for I didn't shrink from declaring all God's message (God's total counsel) to you." In other words, His expectations are that whatever we choose should be in line with God's divine will for our lives. On the surface, it could seem weak and unskillful for someone to not make a decision without first of all knowing what the mind of God is concerning the situation. On the contrary, it proves and demonstrates strength, trust and confidence in the supreme and only one God, which is what scripture admonishes us: …"For he that cometh to God must believe He is, and rewards those who diligently seek Him (Hebrews 11:6)." Seeking Him is knowing what His counsel for your life is, and living according to it. "Your ears will hear sweet words behind you: Go this way. There is your path; this is how you should go. Whenever you must decide whether to turn to the right or the left. (Isaiah 30:21 TVB)".

It is imperative for an individual who wants to cultivate a leadership (overcoming) spirit to adopt this kind of mindset. An individual once said, "A man is nothing without his God!" Moses also in Exodus 33:15 said that if the presence of the Lord God would not go with them, then they also would not depart an inch. What greatness you could achieve when you learn to make your choices through God! To get this accomplished does not mean that you should become indecisive in the face of life's battles and challenges under the pretext of waiting on God. Absolutely not!

Some of the characteristics of effective leadership are being prompt, being quick to discern the right from the wrong decision when confronted with a problem, and being able to act accordingly. Failure to address the situation promptly could be hazardous to the entire situation. The story is told of two fishermen in the same boat who were going through a serious storm. They could not easily figure out what to do as the boat was being tossed here and there by the strong waves of the sea. In that stupor, one of them asked the other if they should pray or row. The other without any waste of time said, "We must do both". He understood the role of prayer in such a situation, as well as the need to take a prompt decision to keep on doing what they were supposed to do. Unfortunately, nowadays, many have taken prayers as an escape road from doing what they are supposed to. In the same light, in the midst of challenges leaders should do both—and promptly—otherwise they will be tossed to a place of no return. Therefore, in such crucial moments, all you need to do is to pray and ask the Lord for divine wisdom to address the situation. James 1:5 says: "If you want to know what God wants you to do, ask Him, and He will gladly tell you, for He is always ready to give a bountiful supply of wisdom to all who ask Him….(TLB)." A leader needs to ensure that his motives and desires are pure and genuine when making crucial decisions and that they are not for personal gain. He should equally commit his motives/desires into God's hands and the peace of God will rule his heart as he gains enough inspiration and divine wisdom on which direction to take. It was this wisdom and knowledge that King Solomon asked the Lord to give him so that he may know how to govern in justice. He desired to rule the people of Israel in a way that pleased the Lord:

> Solomon replied, O God, you have been so kind and good to my father David, and now you have given me the kingdom – This is all I want … Now give me wisdom and knowledge to rule them properly, for who is able to govern by himself such a great nation as this one of yours (2 Chronicles .1:8-10 TLB)?

It is vital to allow God to choose through you. It is also important to realize that doing so does not contradict your personality and ideas in any way. It rather allows God to reinforce your personality and ideals with His own. It also allows Him to make you stable and unmovable in the battles of life as you make worthwhile and long-standing decisions that will stand the test of time. Remember the scriptures say that they that know their God shall be strong and do great exploits (Daniel 11:32).

Right Decisions And Incoming Storms

Making the right decision (the God kind of decision) does not automatically prevent the storms of life from raging. As long as the heavens and earth remains, storms and challenges would come to test your confidence in the decisions you have taken. It is not time to quit the right decisions because of incoming storms, "...For he that wavereth is like a wave of the sea driven with the wind and tossed. For let not that man think that he shall receive any thing of the Lord (James 1:6, 7)." It is important to view the decisions you make as the "choice of the Lord", and stick with them no matter the surrounding pressures. A man is only known by the ideas he pursues, the decisions he makes, the goals he presses towards, and the assignments he is committed to. These defining factors qualify you to be a mentor and leader over people and circumstances. Remember that quitters don't lead and leaders don't quit. This concept is reiterated throughout scriptures:

- "But we are not of those who draw back to perdition, but of those who believe to the saving of the soul (Hebrews 10:39)."
- "But Jesus told him, 'Anyone who lets himself be distracted from the work I plan for him is not fit for the Kingdom of God' (Luke 9:62)."

Consider an analysis of Moses, the Israelite Exodus and the wilderness experience: Moses and the people were in the desert, but what was he going to do with them? They had to be fed, and that he did. According to Dan's Faithweb, the quarter-master general of the U.S. Army reported that Moses would have provided 1500 tons of food each day. To bring that much food each day, two freight trains – each a mile long – would be required! Besides, you must remember that they were out in the desert, so they would need firewood for cooking. This would take 4000 tons of wood and a few more freight trains – each a mile long – just for one day. And just think: they were 40 years in transit. They would have to have water. If they only had enough to drink and wash a few dishes, it would take 11,000,000 gallons each day, and a freight train with tank cars – 1800 miles long – just to bring it! But then, there is another problem; each time they settled at the end of the day, a camp ground 2/3 the size of Rhode Island was required: 750 square miles. Do you think Moses figured all this out before he left Egypt? I think not! For if he would have figured all these out, he would not just have complained of an impediment in his speech: "Please Lord, I am not a talented speaker. I have never been good with words. I wasn't when I was younger and I haven't gotten any better since you revealed yourself to me. I stutter and stammer. My words get all twisted (Exodus 4:10 TVB)."

He would have rather complained more of the enormity of the assignment as an unrealistic project as he could see that he lacks the physical resources for it. I think he knew it was a great project and all of the finer details needed to be figured out. Yet he trusted the greatness of his God. Often times, leaders quit because they concern themselves with trying to get every detail and the feasibility of the projects rather than depending on Him with Whom nothing is impossible: "For with God nothing will be impossible (Luke1:37)." Irrespective of the mammoth size of the projects we pursue, and no matter the series of splashes (failures) and challenges we face, we will see success if we do not give up and keep the faith (God's word). We must continue on in faith until we see the victory.

It is our faith is the victory that overcomes the world (1 John 5:4). This marks the quality of a true leader. Be strong, courageous, effective and show yourself worthy. This was the counsel David gave to Solomon who was the new king of Israel in 1Chronicles 28: 20. David assured him that the Eternal God will never leave nor abandon him until he had finished the work assigned to him of the Lord. This means that God will never engage you in a project that He does not intend for you to finish. Beloved, be courageous in the mandate assigned to you. He will be with you till the end. Christ assured the disciples in Matthew 28: 18-20:

> I am here speaking with the authority of God, who has commanded me to give you this commission: Go out and make disciples in all the nations…Then disciple them. Form them in the practices and postures that I have taught you, and show them how to follow the commands I have laid down for you. And I will be with you, day after day, to the end of the age (TVB).

And this same point is emphasized in Hebrews 13:5: …; For Himself has said, "I will never leave you nor forsake you (RKJV)." Divine leadership is a faith issue. All we need to know is where the people are, and where they are supposed to be at what time. All other factors, our desires, and the impossible, are left to God as we step out in faith. When we do step out, we can then know that the details are good. Scripture says, "No one ever builds a house without first calculating the cost (Luke 14:28)." Do not be fearful or discouraged, just step out in faith.

Assessing Your Level Of Assurance In God's Decisions

Every Christian believes God, but how long they continue believing Him depends on the level of assurance they have in Him. It is not God's decision that easily develops a leadership and conquering attitude, but the assurance you have in it. This alone would subsequently influence your corresponding actions. Your degree of assurance and confidence in God's decision for your life will determine your standing on them, and will consequently determine the totality of how you would carry yourself.

If you wish to develop a conquering and leadership spirit in God, you need to get to a point of perfect assurance in God that whatever His decisions are would be the best and would be realized come-what-may. It is at this point, that you will be able to give a ready answer to any question posed by any confused individual, even as Paul wrote in his second letter to Timothy: "….Nevertheless I am not ashamed; for I know whom I have believed, and am persuaded that he is able to keep that which I have committed unto him against that day (2 Timothy 1:12)." Beloved, do you really know the God whom you have believed? If you do, then you would joyfully lay down your own desires and decisions for His. Paul knew it will not take himself but God to bring out the best of his life. No doubt he was fully persuaded in God, which becomes a challenge for most of us.

Consider God's Word To Be 'Yes and Amen!'

This is a very sensitive point when it comes to cultivating a leadership (overcoming) spirit, for a man is only as strong as the God he serves. We must grow to a point that we no longer take God's Word lightly but take it for what it says and act on it in the way that it demands from us. Consider the text below:

> For ye have heard of my conversation in time past in the Jew's religion, how that beyond measure I persecuted the church of God, and wasted it. And profited in the Jews' religion above many of my equals in mine own nation, being more exceedingly zealous of the traditions of my fathers. But

when it pleased God, who separated me from my mother's womb, and called me by his grace, to reveal his Son in me, that I might preach him among the heathen; immediately I conferred not with flesh and blood: neither went I up to Jerusalem to them which were apostles before me; but I went into Arabia, and returned again unto Damascus. (Galatians 1:13-17).

Before the Apostle Paul became a partaker of the faith, he was a part of the Jewish religion and a very successful individual in it as well. He was exceedingly zealous about it as well and got himself actively involved in persecuting the church of God with an intense hatred for Christians. Take note that when the Lord finally revealed Jesus to him and how he was going to become a preacher of that which he persecuted, he did not confer with flesh and blood, neither did he seek for the opinions of the apostles, nor the opinions of his fellow Jewish colleagues. Instead, he gave himself over to God to become what He would have him to be. Paul indeed was quite quick to respond to the call of God upon this life, and did that early enough. During this time he put aside every form of distraction and went into a period of retreat in Arabia where he received spiritual fortification from the Lord. This made him apt to respond and execute the call upon his life. Many today, even when they identify their call, are slow to respond as they seek to have all unnecessary questions answered first.

This strong belief and confidence in God's Word became the inner strength in Paul and automatically defined his new lifestyle. This included the way he spoke, what he would and would not tolerate from people, etc. To sum this up, his personality and ideals were transformed by his encounter with Jesus. The same thing will eventually happen to you if you consider every word of God as "Yes and Amen". That is if you do not question His word, but receive it just as He says it. We need to get to a point that we can boldly stand for what we believe in without allowing room for fear, threats or bashfulness. Someone once said, "It is a criminal offence to be ashamed of that which you believe in.'' Paul says in 2 Timothy 1:8-9, "Be not thou therefore ashamed of the testimony of our Lord…but be thou partaker of the affliction of the gospel according to the power of God; who hath saved us, and called us with a holy calling…." This must be how much one should endure for the faith he believes in—even in afflictions—without compromise of any of its virtues. This emboldens his spirit, making him tough as he faces the realities of life.

Get Rid Of Every Escapist Mentality

It is important to realize that in your daily life, there are events and circumstances that you would encounter which are unavoidable no matter how spiritual you may be. In such cases, the manner in which you handle such moments is worth noting. This is because, more often than not,

God wants to teach us lessons which we might never have been taught; even as it pleased the Lord that Christ should grow like a plant taking root out of dry ground (Isaiah 53:2). As such, we must be able to manage ourselves as we understand the mind of God towards us. This will help us to address circumstances, enable us to stand our ground, and not give up by looking for possible means to escape situations beyond our control. The determination to courageously stand firm even in the midst of turbulence builds within us a largeness of heart and a supernatural ability to withstand pressure of all kinds. Paul himself went through such moments and was tempted to escape even as it is written:

> And lest I should be exalted above measure through the abundance of the revelations, there was given to me a thorn in the flesh, the messenger of Satan to buffet me, lest I should be exalted above measure. For this thing I besought the Lord thrice, that it might depart from me. And he said unto me, my grace is sufficient for thee for my strength is made perfect in weakness… (2 Corinthians. 12:7-9).

In struggling to escape such situations, Paul pleaded with the Lord thrice, but all he got in response was, "My grace is sufficient... my strength is made perfect in weakness (vs. 9)". This response alone had the ability to build within him resistance against all the wiles and storms of life. This knowledge makes one to become 'petros' which is founded on 'petra' (i.e. a little stone which is founded upon a mighty rock such that it can't be plucked out). As seen in scriptures: "And I also say to you that you are Peter (petros) and on this rock (petra) I will build my church, and the gates of Hades shall not prevail against it (Matthew 16:18)." Therefore, every time we rest upon the Lord as we go through the storms of life, His strength and grace becomes more evident in us and we will overcome supernaturally what others are easily overcome by in the natural. Such were the testimonies of Shadrach, Meshach, and Abednego in the furnace of fire (Daniel 3:14-30), and Daniel in the Lion's den (Daniel 6).

Chapter Three

THE POWER TO TAKE ON RESPONSIBILITIES

There is no proof of maturity and leadership without the ability to take on responsibilities. It is impossible to practically express oneself and one's potentials without executing certain duties. What most people are afraid of when taking on responsibilities is the anticipation of the challenges involved. It is actually a courageous venture and it would take a courageous individual to face it. This differentiates a leader or champion from a failure. It was Abraham's spiritual maturity and his ability to handle life's issues that earned him the trust of the Lord. The Lord entrusted into his hands what the scripture writes: "…I have made thee a father of many nations … who against hope believed in hope, that he might become the father of many nations … (Romans 4:17,18)."

The above scripture reveals to us what qualified Abraham to take on such responsibility and become a father to nations—his largeness of heart and confidence in God. He did not allow his hope in God to be limited to what is seen, but on what is not seen. Against all hope or logic, he hoped. You need to apply the same principle if you are to take up certain responsibilities. You must stop seeing things as everybody else does, and rather, start hoping towards the end result you want to see. It is the ability to see beyond the natural that defines leadership.

The Importance Of Taking On Responsibilities

It is worth noting that chaos and anarchy would become natural if fear of taking on responsibilities become the order of our lives. Paul emphasized this role to Titus when he wrote: "To Titus, mine own son after the common faith … For this cause left I thee in Crete, that thou shouldest set in order the things that are wanting, and ordain elders in every city, as I had appointed thee (Titus 1:4-5)." Taking on and delegating responsibility in any sector of life has the ability to maintain order. It also must be realized that it demonstrates an "autarky". An autarky is an economic term that demonstrates a system of self-sufficiency. Paul admonished Titus in Titus 1:9, to hold firmly to the trustworthy message as it has been taught, so that he can encourage others by sound doctrine and refute those who oppose it. Titus could only execute such responsibilities based on how well and illuminated he was in his inward man (i.e. a kind of inward authority in that domain).

It is now time we become responsible to the point that darkness no longer characterizes our lives nor our immediate environment. This will require that we have a certain degree of understanding of certain issues, coupled with the desire to see change. Someone once said: "A man's greatest mountain is his own ignorance''. It is time we awake and take heed of Isaiah 33:6: "And wisdom and knowledge shall be the stability of thy times…This is the sure ground of success and it is at this platform of wisdom and knowledge that creativity is birthed." Hence, taking on responsibilities becomes the immediate outcome.

Preparation For Responsibilities

Being able to take on responsibilities is very vital if one must be able to influence the world around them. You must therefore build up and prepare yourself for such a task. One of the major ways of getting yourself equipped to face this task is studying widely—especially in the domain in that you want to become relevant in. For it is written: "Study to show thyself approved unto God, a workman that needeth not to be ashamed, rightly dividing the word of truth (2 Timothy 2:15)." Studying is an important factor when you want to take on responsibilities. This qualifies you as an individual to execute these responsibilities well. It is also important to realize that knowledge has an ability to do away with every form of inferiority complex in the life of the individual concerned. It then equally causes him to stick out his neck above the heads of the multitude as he, without any need for shame, takes on certain challenging responsibilities. It is time to prioritize the art of studying and building up yourself if you want relevance and significance. Scripture says: "Wisdom is the principal thing; therefore get wisdom: and with all thy getting get understanding (Proverbs 4:7)."

2 Timothy 3:16 writes: "All scripture is given by inspiration of God, and is profitable for doctrine, for reproof, for correction, for instruction in righteousness: that the man of God may be perfect, thoroughly furnished unto all good works." That was equally the secret of Jesus' success; "tactfulness and skilfulness" in His ministerial adventures on earth, even as it is said of Him, "…Lord, I come (in the volume of the book it is written of me) to do thy will, O God (Hebrews 10:7)." He who reads leads, and he who leads reads. The art of studying is therefore the challenge

thrown to every individual who wants to become a leader and who wants to stay relevant and significant in life as he daily faces new challenges in an evolving world.

A Word To Teachers

There will always be problems to solve and issues to be addressed which we cannot afford to ignore. Abraham Lincoln, former US president, wrote a letter to a headmaster in a school in which his son was studying:

> He will have to learn, I know, that all men are not just and are not true. But teach him if you can the wonder of books … but also give him quiet time to ponder the external mystery of birds in the sky, bees in the sun and flowers on a green hillside; teach him it is far more honourable to fail than to cheat… Teach him to have faith in his own ideas, even if everyone tells him he is wrong. Teach him to be gentle with gentle people and tough with the tough. Try to give my son the strength not to follow the crowd when everyone is getting on the bandwagon…Teach him to listen to all men; but teach him also to filter all he hears on a screen of truth, and take only the good that comes through. Teach him, if you can, how to laugh when he is sad…Teach him there is no shame in tears. Teach him to scoff at cynic and to beware of too much sweetness… Teach him to sell his brawn and brain to highest bidders, but never to put a price on his heart and soul. Teach him to close his ears to a howling mob …and stand and fight if he thinks he is right. Treat him gently, but do not cuddle him, because only the test of fire makes fine steel. Let him have the courage to be impatient … Let him have the patience to be brave. Teach him always to have sublime faith in himself, because then he will have faith in humankind. This is a big order, but see what you can do... He is such a fine little fellow my son!

From this letter by Abraham Lincoln, we learn the following:

1) In the pursuit of studies, studying widely even on things that may not be too related towards what we are geared at is of great importance also. It gives a broader spectrum of life and makes us to view life from a mountain (superiority perspective).

2) Believe in your own ideas and potentials and execute them even if you fail, rather than just wait for others to set the pace for you. Otherwise, you'll not leave your own footprints of life that others can follow.

3) We must learn to be flexible and not rigid so we can be able to handle people of all temperaments. This confirms what Paul said of himself: "To the weak became I as weak, that I might gain the weak; I am made all things to all men, which I might by all means save some (1 Corinthians 9:22).

4) We should never give up as we press on making our marks, irrespective of the erasers waiting to confront us. For unless we're willing to take the bull by its horns, we wouldn't be able to grow our own horns.

5) It is never too early to teach a child virtues and values of life.

6) Raising up a child demands more than one person's contribution. Expose the child to the right instructors and right ideas.

Chapter Four

ZERO TOLERANCE

*T*here is harmony and inner peace to be found in following a moral compass that points in the same direction, regardless of fashion or trend (Ted Koppel)."

At One time, coach Davis of Miami told his assistant coaches that in recruiting, "They will be forgiven for making a talent mistake, but they will be fired for making a character mistake". He said "There's no excuse for character errors", and that those recruited must be of a noble character. He was preparing young men to win not only in football games, but more importantly, to win in life. What a great leader coach Davis was. Although he was interested in getting the best talents, he would not do so at the expense of character. Character will keep you elevated for a lifetime, while talent can only do so for a moment. So many great leaders who could have been role-models for generations to come were cut because of character issues. In fact, a former president of the International Monetary Fund (IMF) and would-be contestant for the presidency of France by the name of Dominic Strauss Kahn had to resign his candidacy due to character issues. He was accused of rape and could no longer contest for the presidency.

The unfortunate thing is that these character issues are not only the challenges of worldly leaders, but even servants of the Lord. It is quite disheartening to know that there are so many ministers of the Gospel who became indifferent when their characters were challenged—not only in their personal lives, but in relation to others. They have ignored addressing certain compromising issues and behaving as though all is well when it was not really the case. As such, they have lost the respect of the people and consequently the possibility of effectively ministering to them. They are now seen as ordinary and mere men of no worth.

Beloved in the Lord, it is interesting to note that the reason why most ministries have developed this degree of unhealthy tolerance is because they think that if they become a little stricter, their flock may abandon them. I don't mean to say we need to become unnecessarily hard; rather, we may rationalize our dealing with people in a way which does not compromise the issue of sin. Realize that in Jesus' prayer for Peter in Luke 22:31-32, He said; "when thou art converted, strengthen thy brethren." For this to be possible, Peter needed to become a little hard disciplined in his dealings with them. Consider the letter of Paul to his spiritual son Titus below:

> Holding fast the faithful word as he hath been taught, that he may be able by sound doctrine both to exhort and to convince the gainsayers. For there are many unruly and vain talkers and deceivers, especially they of the circumcision: Whose mouths must be stopped, who subvert whole houses, teaching things which they ought not, for filthy lucre's sake. One of themselves, even a prophet of their own, said, The Cretians are always liars, evil beast, and slow bellies. This witness is true. Therefore rebuke them sharply, that they may be sound in the faith (Titus 1:9-13).

Paul taught Titus how to handle people who compromised the gospel for their own selfish gain, as well as those living with hidden sin: that he should vehemently and sharply rebuke them. This is precisely how we can set the Christian standard, by not tolerating questionable habits or characteristics.

Beloved, we are dealing with a disciplined and a strict God who does not tolerate any form of sin. Scripture warns that friendship with the world is enmity with God (James 4:4). Refusing to compromise when it comes to God's standards is a serious issue that deserves our attention. We must treat it with great vexation of spirit. Sin indeed is our enemy and we must draw the battle line against it. As we develop a strong hatred against sin, so also, are we simultaneously cultivating a leadership spirit. This leadership spirit then creates within us a degree of boldness and authority as we address certain issues. Hebrews 1:8-9 says: "… a sceptre of righteousness is the sceptre of thy kingdom, (for) thou hast loved righteousness, and hated iniquity…." Notice here that righteousness and hatred of sin puts in one's hands a sceptre and a domain of influence (a sceptre refers to rulership and authority). How many of us will be able to rule in our society and world? It is time, beloved in the Lord, that we draw a demarcation between us and sin, just as Abraham said to the rich man who was tormented in hell that he could not come over to his side to give him water because of a big pit separating them as recorded in Luke 16:22-26:

> Now it came to pass, that the beggar died, and was carried by the angels into Abraham's bosom. The rich man also died, and was buried. And in Hades he lifted up his eyes, while in torments. And he saw Abraham far away and Lazarus in his bosom. Then he cried and said, "Father Abraham, have mercy on me, and send Lazarus so that he may dip the tip of his finger in water and cool my tongue, for I am tormented in this flame". But Abraham said "Son, remember that in your lifetime, you received your good things, and likewise Lazarus evil things. But now he is comforted and you are

suffering. "And beside all this, between us and you there is a great gulf fixed, so that they who wish to come over from here to you cannot, nor can those from there cross over to us".

So also is supposed to be the degree of our demarcation with sin. For righteousness sets in an individual an uncompromising standard for godliness, hence authority. A man who can ignore the ungodly and compromising habits of others is a man who, himself, is a hidden sinner. Consider this sign on a Baltimore church building "All trespassers shall be prosecuted to the full course of the law. Signed: the Sisters of Mercy." Wow! This therefore means that mercy doesn't mean tolerance or compromise with evil. We must cultivate such a leadership attitude in order to make the crooked paths straight. We must see to it that evil does not dwell in our neighborhood (1Thesalonians 5:15). Paul admonished Timothy in 2 Timothy 4:23 to "preach the Word; be instant in season, out of season; reprove, rebuke, exhort with all longsuffering and doctrine; for the time will come when they will not endure sound doctrine."

Never Be Discouraged

In as much as we cultivate such a leadership spirit which is bent on setting the standard of holiness and discipline for greater success in life, ministry and career, we must be able to sustain within ourselves a certain degree of patience until we witness the expected change in the lives of those we are hoping to influence. The scripture above (2 Timothy 4:2-3) says that though we may reprove and rebuke, yet we must also be able to exhort with all long-suffering and doctrine. This portrays immense love and patience (though seemingly unpleasing) and continual teaching until all the anticipated be met with. Our degree of love and patience illustrates how big we are on the inside.

A story is told of a 35 year-old man who was still living with his father. One day, he was struggling to feed their little pig because it was excitedly moving up and down the fence. He then became so irritated with the piglet that he began to beat it. He beat the little pig until he finally broke its leg. The pig cried the whole day long. When his father returned and found out what happened, he said to his son, "Do you see why I said you are not yet ready for marriage? If you could get that angry and impatient with a piglet for what is but obvious, what then would you do to a lady who truly will annoy you any time on one thing or the other?" Beloved, patience and love are necessary as we desire to rebuke every evil action. With these in place, we must then become instant both in and out of season to set orderliness at whatever cost: "These things speak, and exhort and rebuke with all authority. Let no man despise thee (Titus 2:15)."

Even when it does seem like we are failing, discouragement should never creep into our hearts, for quitters never win and winners never quit. Michael Jordan –arguably the greatest basketball player ever—testified this of himself: "I've missed more than 9000 shots in my career. I've lost almost 300 games. 26 times I've been trusted to take the game-winning shot…and missed. I have failed over and over and over again in my life. And that is why I succeeded." Discouragement has always been what great heroes refused to tolerate in their hearts irrespective of how much they failed. Our passion to the vision is going to wear away every discouraging factor, causing us to triumph everyday in our pursuit of purpose. In fact, one of the greatest American presidents Abraham Lincoln once said during a civil war, "I do the very best I know how; the very best I can; and I mean to keep on doing it to the end. If the end brings me out all right, what is said against me will not amount to anything. If the end brings me out all wrong, then a legion of angels swearing I was right will make no difference."

Great leaders have always been those who have fought for positive changes irrespective of the pressure against them. They have always been those who didn't set on their mission for the quest of fame or popularity. Neither are fame and popularity the measuring rods for great leaders. They set out for a deadly mission and fame came chasing them. Courage indeed is a necessary quality for true leadership, and only through it can leaders press forward their innovative ideas.

It is the same way Nelson Mandela, commonly known as Madiba, of The Republic of South Africa, fought against white domination over the blacks. He was imprisoned for 27 years and when they proposed to release him on basis that he stop his freedom fighting, he refused. It is noted of him that he said, "I have cherished a democratic and free society where citizens do have equal opportunities and rights, and which people will not be judged by the colour of their skin but by the content of their character." He said these were ideas he was willing to live for, and that if need be, these were ideas he was ready to die for. He fought for this irrespective of threats and prevailed. When he finally was released and eventually sworn in as president in 1994, he forgave his oppressors. At his death in December 5, 2013, the current President of South Africa by name Jacob Zuma said of him, "Our nation has lost its greatest son." I thought the President would have said, "Our nation has lost its greatest prisoner." This means that irrespective of the shame and humiliation you may suffer because of your pursuit of justice in leadership, you will not be defined by shame, but by your success. Fight until you win. At his funeral, more than 100 world presidents, the secretary general of United Nations, and other dignitaries were present. It should be noted that world changers refuse to let losses dictate their future; they continue to persevere until they win.

Chapter Five

BUILDING UP A LEADERSHIP SPIRIT

𝔇early beloved, having come this far, it is important to know how to build (cultivate) a leadership spirit. Unless we cultivate such a spirit and live by it, influence in Christianity would be quite shallow and our footprints would not be visible and will eventually disappear with the passing of time. As we proceed to learn how to build such a leadership spirit, we need to first of all understand what it basically is all about.

Leadership Spirit

To be a little more precise and practical, "leadership spirit" depicts a certain level of wisdom, maturity, and experience in specific issues dealing with humanity and society. It will implant in him a certain degree of understanding and knowledge that will result in a greater level of excitement and zeal when handling life's issues. This should be to an extent that it evokes from the individual mere excitement and zeal concerning life's issues as it implants in him a certain degree of understanding and knowledge. This becomes in him an inward drive as he becomes much more practical as he handles life's issues. Such an individual is fully equipped mentally and psychologically, and is therefore a perfect example of one who has dealt away with certain unruly emotions, especially when it comes to being real to life in making and standing on certain decisions. They may even have some emotional feelings and concerns relating to certain issues, but this does not affect their rational minds, as they would not allow themselves to be influenced by such. This precisely is due to their experience of the past. Such individuals have come a long way through life that they can't afford compromising on certain issues. This is true of Jesus as the scriptures say, "Although He was a son, Jesus learned obedience through the things He suffered (Hebrews 5:8)."

This whole idea of a leadership spirit can be portrayed in the text of scripture from

1 Corinthians 13:11: When I was a child, I spake as a child, I understood as a child, I thought as a child: but when I became a man, I put away childish things. Realize from this testimony of Paul that he made a clear distinction between two different phases of his life: an immature stage and a matured stage. It is important to note that he, in talking about when he was a child, doesn't mean when he was yet young in terms of age. Rather, he meant when he was spiritually immature. As we can therefore learn from his life, it is quite clear that there are many spiritually immature adults today in the Body of Christ. Irrespective of their number of years in the faith, their speech and manner of life betrays their years. It is therefore important for us to cultivate a matured and fatherly way of life if our significance would be relevant. It is also necessary to note that a leadership (fatherly) spirit has a very high ability to discern into issues that an ordinary Christian may not be able to (though the Christian may be full of the Holy Spirit and may even have the gifts of discernment of spirits). Paul said concerning the leadership he was submitted to: "And when James, Cephas and John, who seemed to be pillars, perceived the grace that was given unto me, they gave to me and Barnabas the right hand of fellowship; that we should go on to the heathen, and they unto the circumcision. Let us go for this (Galatians 2:9)."

Know Your Limits As You Promote The Strengths Of Others

Looking at Galatians 2:9 above, those who were pillars perceived the special grace of the Lord upon the lives of Paul and Barnabas. They were quite pleased with God's hand upon them and did all they could to ensure that Paul and Barnabas succeed in their ministry. By so doing, they gave them the right hand of fellowship. They recognized their value and importance as well as their maturity. This right hand of fellowship was their approval before the church and confirmation of the fact that their ministry was of the Lord. This gave Paul and Barnabas credibility before the saints. They commissioned them to the heathen, where their mandate needed expression the most, while they remained with the Jews.

Real leadership is not intimidated when others have particular strengths which they may lack. Neither should a subordinate be proud because he is specially gifted in some areas above his superiors; he must stay submissive to authority. Once a leader can identify such particular strengths in others, it becomes wise to position them at the right areas where their gifting can have expressions. Only then will the subordinates stay loyal, without which, he may rebel against his authorities as he sees them as obstructions to his destiny. Samuel Eto'o Fils, a former captain for the Cameroonian National Football Team (The Indomitable Lions) is a prime example. When he was first taken to Europe and bought by Real Madrid (one of the world's top division one soccer team in Spain) was hardly featuring on the field. Rather, he was always on the reserved bench.

This team eventually lighted him to another division one team in Spain (Real Mallorca). There he was allowed to play, except for when Mallorca was to play Real Madrid. Eventually, Real Madrid sold him to Barcelona. There his talents and potentials were given opportunity to be expressed. He emerged as a world football star and earned the title of the best goal scorer in Spain (Pichichi) many times. He ensured every time he was to play against Real Madrid that he did his best to score. He hated Real Madrid and never wanted to play for them again because he said they wanted to kill his talents by not giving him the opportunity to express it. By giving people the opportunity to express their gifting, their passion increases and they will be more willing to take the challenge for more exploits. The passion within Paul for the ministry is similar to what Jeremiah said about the word of God being like fire in his bones: Then I said, "I will not make mention of Him, nor speak anymore in His name. But His word was in my heart like a burning fire shut up in my bones; I was weary of holding it back, and I could not (Jeremiah 20:9)." Paul cautioned Timothy not to neglect the gifts in him, but to put them to work:

> These things command and teach. Let no man despise your youth. Be an example to the believers, in word, in behaviour, in love, in spirit, in faith, in purity. Till I come, give heed to reading, to exhortation, to teaching. Do not neglect the gift that is in you, which was given to you by prophecy with the laying on of the presbytery, meditate on these things. Give yourself wholly to them so that your progress may appear to all (1Timothy 4:11-15).

How To Cultivate A Leadership Spirit

To begin with, there are two different approaches to cultivating the spirit of leadership. First and foremost, we must admit the fact, as discussed earlier, that a leadership spirit is that of an exemplary way of life for the rest to follow. For it to be cultivated, the backbone or strength behind it are certain laid down virtues, as demonstrated in the text below:

> These things command and teach. Let no man despise thy youth; but be thou an example of the believers, in word, in conversation, in charity, in spirit, in faith, in purity … Give attendance to reading, to exhortation, to doctrine: Neglect not the gift that is in thee… Meditate upon these things; give thyself wholly to them, that thy profiting may appear to all…Continue in them: for in doing this thou shalt both safe thyself and them that hear thee (1Timothy 4:11-16).

a.   The Foundational Approach

This was precisely the counsel Brother Paul gave to his spiritual son Timothy. He taught him things that would give him a firm foundation as a leader. He told Timothy the things which he had to command and teach. But he made him understand that if that was going to be effective, he had to first of all be an example of such things. Paul urged him to be an example in word, conversation, charity, spirit, faith and purity.

These virtues enlisted above are the most essential an individual must cultivate in his life if he desires to become an example and a leader for others to follow, i.e. a mentor. Realize that each of the virtues above communicate and illustrate the following:

i.   Word—wisdom and knowledge
ii.   Conversation—integrity and interaction
iii.   Charity—ability to show kindness
iv.   Spirit—maturity
v.   Faith—confidence in God
vi.   Purity--Soundness of life style

The level to which our life reflects each of these qualities will set us as the leaders, mentors and role models that others can follow. Therefore, it is very important for us to cultivate such virtues, even as Philippians 4:8 writes: "Finally, brethren, whatsoever things are true, whatsoever things are honest, whatsoever things are just, whatsoever things are pure, whatsoever things are lovely, whatsoever things are of good report, if there be any virtue, and if there be any praise, think on these things." As we prayerfully meditate upon and practice these virtues, the more they're being built in us, setting us up for public significance and relevance. Then our profiting will eventually appear to all. In fact, leaders don't fight to lead. They just be themselves, doing what they are supposed to do, and they will eventually discover a great number of followers looking up to them.

b.   *The Consummative Approach*

After having laid down the foundation above, the challenge now lies in the consummative step. While the foundation has to do with building up and equipping oneself for leadership, the consummative step involves the practical application of a leadership spirit to everyday life. Realize that Paul as earlier seen in 1Timothy 4:11, commanded Timothy that he must command and teach the others. This is quite challenging because in the consummative process of commanding and teaching, people's feelings are often not regarded and may even be trampled upon in the process. This is especially the case when there are issues to be handled that many would find difficult to handle. If such an individual becomes overly consumed with preserving the feelings of others more than the execution of sound judgement, then such an individual is not yet qualified to be a leader and mentor.

Realize that appropriate knowledge and understanding of divine thoughts brings a very strong hatred for every form of unrighteousness and disorder. Consequently, it would entail an individual to become authoritative and commanding; to bark at every disorder and not compromise, especially when the virtues of God are at stake. 2 Corinthians 10:6 says: "And having a readiness to revenge (punish) all disobedience...." Leaders must be bold enough to take corresponding actions. Initially, there may be the fear in the individual's heart to be this commanding, especially when he struggles to consider what the peoples' opinions could be. But in as much as he continues to stand upon the divine virtues as Paul encouraged Timothy, the multitude will have no option but to succumb—even against their own feelings. In 1 Thessalonians 2:10-12, it is written:

> Ye are witnesses and God also, how holily and justly and unblameably we behaved ourselves among you that believe. As ye know how we exhorted and comforted and charged every one of you, as a father doth his children, that ye would walk worthy of God, who hath called you unto his kingdom and glory.

This is so because a righteous life contains and executes the highest authority that there is. Beloved, tow this line, for it is only in you towing this line that you will be able to save both yourself and your hearers. It is very dangerous to understand these truths and not execute them. The Lord warned Prophet Ezekiel in Ezekiel 3:18-19:

> When I say unto the wicked, thou shalt surely die, and thou givest him not warning, nor speaketh to warn the wicked from his wicked way, to save his life; the same wicked man shall die in his iniquity; but his blood will I require at thine hand. Yet if thou warn the wicked and he turn not from his wickedness ... he shall die in his iniquity; but thou hast delivered thy soul.

It is important as leaders and as fathers to play our roles adequately, it is necessary for the fathers to correct the younger generations and to push them towards stirring their gifts and potentials as Paul did to Timothy. Let us identify their potentials and awaken them towards maximizing it, for this is one of the greatest characteristics and responsibilities of a leader towards the younger and unexperienced generations.

Chapter Six

THE POWER OF STAYING FOCUSED

*T*here is a difference between interests and commitment. When you are interested in doing something, you only do it when it is convenient. When you are committed to doing something, you accept no excuses, only results" (Kenneth Blanchard).

This is a vital ingredient in leadership. But this also is where many people have failed in their pursuit of becoming great leaders. Lack of decisiveness or focus has caused more failures than lack of intelligence or ability. There is always that temptation of trying to handle several things at the same time, or the quest for mobility. But as far as leadership is concerned, it will often require us to stick to something longer than we would have wanted to stay. David understood the power of focusing on what he was pressing for. Just as he purposed in his heart; "one thing have I desired of the Lord, that will I seek after: that I may dwell in the house of the Lord all the days of my life, to behold the beauty of the Lord, and to inquire in his temple (Psalm 27:4)." This is a very important portion of scripture on the subject of staying focused. It contains wholesome principles which we can personally adopt. They link together well and will help us, as we aspire to become great leaders, who will set the pace and become pathfinders to later generations. These principles are discussed below:

Understand Who You Are

This is the basic and preliminary factor to consider when you have the drive and focus to pursue something worthwhile. Many people do not know who they really are. Knowing yourself and understanding your personality has a direct link with understanding why you were born and the purpose for which God called you into the ministry. It is only with this understanding that you will be able to carry yourself and know which projects to actually get involved in. As for Jesus, He understood His purpose for coming into the world as He said of Himself: "For the Son of man is come to seek and to save that which was lost (Luke 19:10)." No doubt, everything that defined His daily life and ministry involved that one purpose. Whether it was healing a sick person, teaching the disciples, feeding the multitude, sleeping in the house of a publican, dining with a sinner, journeying on a boat, or going to the cross, etc. Each of these was geared towards accomplishing His purpose.

Understanding the Seasons of Your Life

Having understood who you are, it is then your responsibility to know and to understand the seasons in which you are. Remember, the scriptures declare that "to everything there is a season, and a time to every purpose under the heaven (Ecclesiastes 3:1)". Therefore, every moment defines what specifically needs to be done. We cannot afford to venture into everything at any given time. It takes maturity and discernment to understand the timing for everything we engage in. This is because everything is only going to be fruitful and productive in its season. Solomon in this text was talking about the awareness of time. He knew that, that was the right time to pursue that which he desired. Every time we do not understand seasons and timings for particular issues about our lives and ministries, we will get into unavoidable leadership crisis.

Identify What You Need To Do

Now that you know who you are and that the timing is right, this timing would give you an indication as to what activities you would need to engage in. If you are unable to identify the timing, this will lead to you being unable to identify what you need to do at the time. Purpose and vision will determine the goals to be achieved and what needs to be done to achieve the goals. We have to fully depend on the Holy Spirit who will guide us into what goals we should pursue to realize the vision of the ministry. One major responsibility of a leader is to be able to break down his goals for the entire year into achievable daily, weekly, and monthly fractions. We need to know what our daily targets are and give our all in accomplishing them.

If we cannot break down the goals to daily achievable fractions, then accomplishing the goals set for the year would be a mere myth. When we do succeed into breaking the goals to daily portions, we can easily assess whether we are succeeding in the daily goals or not. If, for any reason, we fail in achieving the goals for a particular day, we must prayerfully repent, assess ourselves and analyze the reasons for which these goals were not achieved. We should then strategize and amend our goals to make it achievable. Unless we approach it this way, with complete focus and hard work, success will be a mere illusion.

There was once a nurse by name Florence Nightingale (1820-1910), who made nursing a genuine profession. She learned not to take "No" for an answer. She worked round the clock in the hospital and became known as the "Lady with the lamp". She later became seriously sick. Queen Victoria wrote in admiration of her efforts: "I wish she were at the war office". Florence wrote a thousand-page document titled "Notes on matters affecting the health, efficiency and hospital administration of the British Army". Although she spent the last 50 years of her life in a sickbed and finally died in 1910, lessons of commitment, focus, and hard-work were drawn from her life, and echoes to eternity. Genuine leaders, though they die, will indisputably live on through the principles and character displayed in their lifetime. If leaders will follow the examples of such great leaders, they will be on a journey to success and every goal will be easily realized.

Know How To Manage Your Desires

Identifying what one needs will eventually usher one to a point of desire. In other words, once a need is identified, a desire will then be generated. This is unavoidable as desires will begin jumping in our hearts just as electrons within an atom. These desires come simultaneously. It is important that they are managed properly, with total reliance on God for success. Even when you have understood the one thing you need to do, it does not prevent similar desires from forming. Contrary desires, which may seem equally promising at the time, may also creep into your heart. Many have found themselves in such situations and the outcome was confusion. The result is then that they embark passionately on one particular desire, but then by the time they have followers who are willing to see the realization of that dream; they have quit and picked up some other cause. This is a sign of immature leadership and will eventually result in discouraged followers who are reluctant to commit.

Know Where And How To Get Your Goals Met

This becomes the next challenge when all the above principles have been set in place. We must realize from the text in Psalm 27:4 that David knew that only in the house of the Lord will he get all the inquiries and counsels that he needed. It is critically important to understand this point. The unfortunate thing with most leaders today is pride and the "I have it all'' mentality. God has designed us in a way that we were all created to be dependent on each other to fulfil our God-given goals: Genesis 2:18 declares: "And the Lord God said, it is not good that the man should be alone. I will make a help meet for him." Note that Eve was not created primarily for the purpose of providing Adam with pleasure or children, but to be a helper (supporter) for the fulfilment of his divine assignment. This should be the determining factor in your criteria for a marriage partner! All leaders need a "helpmeet" for their various assignments. This "helpmeet" may take on the form of input from our fellow colleagues, books written by ministers, or seminars and conferences organized by other ministers. We should be humble enough to glean from others and find solutions. The reason for which the angel told Mary (who had just conceived by the Holy Spirit) about Elizabeth being six months pregnant was because he knew that Elizabeth had experienced every challenge that comes with pregnancy and would serve as counsellor and mentor to Mary (Luke 1:26-45). He knew that this would be especially true as she was being troubled by certain physiological changes in her body because of a pregnancy which she could not logically explain.

Be Ready To Dedicate Yourself Entirely To Achieving Your Goals

This is a very powerful principle in maintaining one's focus. Many people may be quite conversant with the five principles listed above, and may have even set everything in place with regards to following them. The problem lies with this sixth principle which is, in my opinion, what more than 75% of Christians today are lacking in. Instead of exercising this principle, people would rather devote themselves completely to pursuing their own self-interest and pleasures—particularly what will increase their financial status. It is not strange nowadays for pastors to close their churches and ministries for "greener pastures", which is often done by through picking up some secular jobs. Because of this, we cannot really experience the power and presence of God as we should. Notice David in the text said "…that I may dwell in the house of the Lord all the days of my life … "How much of our lives do we dedicate to the service of the Lord? Apostle Paul understood the importance of this and therefore admonished his spiritual son (whom he was disciplining in the ministry) to "give attendance to reading, to exhortation, to doctrine … meditating upon the word of God and giving himself wholly to them, so that his profiting may appear to all (1Timothy 4:13-15)." This is one of the major ways of staying focused in ministry and leadership. We must invest passionately, putting our all into that which we do. By so doing, we will get quick, excellent and glorious results, which become a strong and indispensable factor in driving us to maintain focus and commitment.

The End Result Is Worth The Investment

This also is a very pertinent point in helping you to maintain your focus as a leader. If the end result of your leadership efforts will produce a long-lasting result, then you will be empowered to endure the process of achieving your goals. However, if what you want to achieve can't survive a few years, you may easily get tempted to let it go. This is because it would be easier to let go rather than to achieve that which will be short-lived—especially in light of the pains and sacrifice involved in trying to get it. The durability of your goals will greatly influence your attitude in maintaining your commitment and focus. For as long as we are alive, we have to give it our best and cultivate quality leadership. David spent his life pursuing his desire for God's house because he knew that was what he wanted to be all his life. It is time for us to allow this same desire and passion to characterize our lives.

See your Life's Fulfilment Tied to the Realization of your Goals

It is a fact that everyone needs peace, joy and happiness. Notice the attitude of David in Psalm 122:1 concerning the house of the Lord: "I was glad when they said unto me; Let us go into the house of the Lord." His attitude is always that of joy and happiness when it concerns the house of the Lord. This implies that his fulfilment in life, whether physically, emotionally or otherwise was based on that. This also must be a governing principle in you as you pursue your goals as a leader. You must be able to see your life's fulfilment tied to your goal to be able to maintain your focus and willingness to invest financially into the said goal. Consequently, it will motivate you to press on even when every other person backs off or tries to discourage you. This was quite reflective of the twelve disciples of Jesus; when every other person deserted Jesus, they found their life and fulfilment in Him and were willing to abide with Him:

> From that time many of his disciples went back, and walked no more with him. Then said Jesus unto the twelve, will ye also go away? Then Simon Peter answered him, Lord, to whom shall we go? Thou hast the words of eternal life. And we believe and are sure that thou art the Christ, the Son of the living God (John 6:66-69).

Surround Yourself With the Right People

This is a very serious factor irrespective of your zeal to venture out for God. It will be an error for you to think that you are self-sufficient and hence do not need anybody else. Moreover, not everyone who comes around us are the people for the vision. Some people, no matter how close and friendly they are to you, are not needed if the vision must advance. This does not necessarily mean that they are bad. They could be very genuine people with good hearts towards you and they could also be successful ministerially. However, their pattern and way of life may be such that if you bring them closer to yourself and ministry, their behavioural pattern may become a threat both to you as a leader and to your ministry with regard to integrity, trust etc. They could be good neighbours, good relatives, good friends, but not good ministerial associates. Therefore, your dealings with them must be done cautiously, especially with the ministry and leadership in view.

When the teacher and prophets ministered to the Lord in a fast at Antioch, the Holy Spirit said that Barnabas and Saul should be "separated for the work for which they were called (Acts 13:2)." They were being separated from the rest because God had a unique work for them to do in the Gentile world that the others may have not been called for. Though they were all in the work of the ministry, their assignments were different. That does not mean that they could not be close ministerial associates with the others, but the Holy Ghost knows better why He ordered the separation. We should determine what we have been called for and then identify what (although it may not be bad) could be a potential distraction to our ministerial accomplishments. We should then address it immediately and with wisdom.

Scripture alludes to such distractions (weights) when it says: "Therefore, seeing we are also surrounded by so great a cloud of witnesses, let us lay aside every weight... that so easily entangles us (that slows our pace), and let us run with endurance the race that is set before us. (Hebrews 12:1)." Paul and Barnabas were a good pair, probably because when the apostles initially were afraid of Paul and questioned his conversion, Barnabas was the one who trusted him and held his hand, taking him to the apostles:

> Then Saul spent some days with the disciples who were at Damascus. And immediately he preached Jesus in the synagogues, that He is the Son of God. But all who heard him were amazed, and said, "Is this not he who destroyed those who called on this name in Jerusalem, and came here for that intent, that he might bring them bound to the chief priest." But Saul increased in strength and confounded the Jews who dwelt in Damascus, proving that this Jesus is the Christ... And when Saul had come to Jerusalem, he tried to associate with the disciples, but they were all afraid of him, and did not believe that he was a disciple. But Barnabas took him and brought him to the apostles. And he declared to them how he had seen the Lord on the road and that He (Jesus) had spoken to him, and how he had preached boldly in Damascus in the Name of Jesus. (Acts 9:19-27).

Barnabas fully believed that Paul's encounter with Jesus was real and genuine. He believed in the mandate the Lord handed to him and was fully ready to assist him in the realization of it. It was Barnabas' union with Paul, his willingness to support Paul till the end, and his desire to see God's purpose for Paul's life materialize that gave Paul credibility before the rest. He understood Paul's ministry; no doubt the Holy Spirit had chosen him to be a companion to Paul.

David also understood this principle, when he expressed his joy as can be seen in

Psalm 122:1: "I was glad when they said unto me; let us go into the house of the Lord. It was David's desire to be in God's house (Psalm 27:4)." Now he rejoices according to Psalm 122:1 when they told him that they should go to God's house. This therefore means that David surrounded himself with people who had same passion and desire like himself for the house of the Lord. This is vital in keeping your focus on what you intend to achieve. Note that such people will act as a source of encouragement to you when you are downcast. Their courage to press towards their focus regardless of the challenges they also may be facing would be your motivation to follow suit.

Feed Your Passion

This can effectively be done by seeking out materials on that which you desire to achieve. Examples of doing so could be listening to the testimonies of others, reading great and related books, and researching great men who accomplished great things in their time. Such actions will stir into flames your passion for leadership and ministry. Get to know the challenges they faced, their short-comings and experiences, and how they finally made it at the end. This will build your faith to press on with focus knowing that if God did it for them, He would do it for you. For God does not change (Malachi 3:6), nor is He a respecter of persons (Colossians 3:25). What He did for one, He will do for another as long as He is the initiator of the goals. This was one of the secrets of Solomon the King of Israel—he allowed the testimonies of his predecessor, David the former King, to be his reason of hope, success and focus:

> And Solomon went up thither to the brazen altar before the Lord … and offered a thousand burnt offerings upon it. In that night did God appear unto Solomon, and said unto him, ask what I shall give thee. And Solomon said unto God, thou hast showed great mercy unto David my father, and hast made me to reign in his stead. Now, O Lord God, let thy promise unto David my father be established: for thou hast made me King over a people like the dust of the earth in multitude. Give me now wisdom and knowledge that I may go out and come in before this people: for who can judge this people, that is so great? (2 Chronicles 1:6-10).

From this text, one would immediately realize that Solomon knew much about the kingship of David, how he functioned as King, right to the promises which the Lord promised David. He, in fact, had a document of both fulfilled and still to be fulfilled promises. He understood that if David did succeed, it was because he had an intimate relationship with God and because of the wisdom and knowledge about the things of God which operated in him. No doubt Solomon came to God by means of a thousand sacrifices in one night (which is reflective of building an intimate relationship between himself and God). He asked God for wisdom and knowledge for the purpose of executing adequately the ministry the Lord had given him. Studying the biographies of great and godly men can greatly impact the life and ministry of a leader, creating a greater awareness for the God-given assignment. It also ignites passion for dynamic leadership and adds to the renewal and maintaining of the individual's focus on his assignment.

The Glory Of Small Beginnings

Everyone aspiring to be a great leader must be able to properly manage the foundation of his vision. This will, in the long run, determine the degree of progress and success thereof. In the beginning of everything, it is expected of the visionary or leader to have enough faith to see the growth and maturity of the project through to the end. To spectators, the vision may seem quite insignificant and unachievable at conception. The vision's progress and its greatness solely depend on how much focus and attention the visionary is willing to give to it. This will be as a result of how much he believes in it, irrespective of the opinions of critics.

The most difficult moments will be trying to get supporters and partners for the vision. The reason for this is that people are cautious to partner with something at such a stage, because they are not ultimately sure if it will materialize, and also due to the fact that it may demand from them more than they are able to afford or willing to donate. They often see their engagement at this stage as a risk which they are not sure to take. Only those who love you, and want to see your progress at all cost, will dare support your vision with their resources. One thing the leader should rest his hope on is the fact that God never lies, for He who gave the vision is able to bring it to reality. He should not be more concerned with how unfavourable the beginning may seem to be. The scripture clearly states in Job 8:7: "Though thy beginning was small, yet thy latter end should greatly increase." With this hope, the leader's focus will be guaranteed and the anticipated future will soon become a reality. This ability to conceive greatness out of nothing and bring it, within a short period of time, into physical reality, characterizes great leadership, a quality all leaders should seek.

Faith is a characteristic all leaders must possess. It is "calling those things that are not as though they were (Romans 4:17)." It also is "the substance of things hoped for, and the evidence of things not seen (Hebrews 11:1)." By faith, the elders obtained a good report (Hebrews11:2)." When one studies the entire Hebrews 11 which talks of the great men of faith, one will realize that they all had great projects whose feasibilities from the beginning seemed doubtful. But with their faith, they pressed on against all odds and got the victory. No doubt we are told that without faith, it is impossible to please God (Hebrews11:6). Go for it!

Chapter Seven

TAKING YOUR AUTHORITY

The Place Of Authority

*T*here is never true leadership without authority. The leader must be able to command respect and loyalty from his or her followers. If not, it will be practically impossible for the leader to lead them. An important fact to consider when leading is that respect and loyalty from your followers has to be earned. Without having earned the respect and loyalty of followers, you will simply be a dictator and dominate them. This is very wrong and unscriptural. Unfortunately, this is the kind of leadership that is characteristic of many African governments. Although we must never function in leadership following this type of pattern, leadership WITHOUT authority is also counterproductive. This type of "leadership" results in very little being achieved and also the eventual loss of followers who submit to your leadership.

Understanding How Authority Functions

Before examining how possible it is to earn one's authority, it is very important to understand how authority functions. There are many leaders in great positions of leadership, but they end up losing their authority. All the respect and high esteem from the people vanishes into thin air. Let us look at the life of Jesus Christ as documented in the scriptures below:

> Now after that John was put in prison, Jesus came into Galilee, preaching the gospel of the kingdom of God, and saying, the time is fulfilled, and the kingdom of God is at hand: repent ye and believe the gospel. Now as he walked by the Sea of Galilee, he saw Simon and Andrew his brother casting a net into the Sea: for they were fishers. And Jesus said unto them, come ye after me, and I will make you to become fishers of men. And straightway they forsook their nets, and followed him… And they went into Capernaum; and straightway on the Sabbath day he entered into the synagogue, and taught. And they were astonished at his doctrine: for he taught them as one that had authority, and

53

not as the scribes. And there was in their synagogues a man with an unclean spirit; and he cried out, saying, let us alone, what have we to do with thee, thou Jesus of Nazareth? Art thou come to destroy us? I know thee who thou art, the Holy One of God. And Jesus rebuked him, saying, hold thy peace, and come out of him. And when the unclean spirit had torn him and cried with a loud voice, he came out of him. And they were all amazed, in so much that they questioned among themselves, saying, what thing is this? What new doctrine is this? For with authority commandeth he even the unclean spirits, and they do obey him. And immediately his fame spread abroad throughout all region round about Galilee (Mark 1:14-21).

We see from the text above and throughout scripture how Jesus perpetually functioned in authority. This authority attracted many followers and also caused demons to cry out before Jesus uttered a word. This was one of the greatest secrets to His leadership and ministry success. When we examine the above text thoroughly as well as other related texts, there are quite a handful of principles one can emulate with regard to how authority functions:

Know Your Jurisdiction

It must be noted that every authority has a sphere of influence (jurisdiction). It does not matter how much power and authority the US president has; he has no jurisdiction in any other nation except it is permitted by that nation's government. If he is given permission to express authority in that nation, then he may exercise his authority but it will only be under the authority of that nation's president. Spiritually, the same principle applies.

As a leader, you need to know our sphere of influence. If you must stick to the vision the Lord gives you to execute, then all those He brings to submit to the vision will automatically become your sphere of influence. Without this, your authority will be questionable. Jesus in the text could preach the gospel of the kingdom with all authority. He cast the unclean spirit out of the man and this was possible because that was the commission His Father had given Him. He testified in Luke 4:18-19:

> The Spirit of the Lord is upon me, because he hath anointed me to preach the gospel to the poor, he hath sent me to heal the broken-hearted, to preach deliverance to the captives; and recovering of sight to the blind, to set at liberty them that are bruised, to preach the acceptable year of the Lord.

Therefore, your jurisdiction of spiritual authority is determined by your divine assignment. It is also influenced by your understanding of the fact that you are expected to heal the sick, raise the dead, cleanse lepers, etc. everywhere you go (Mark 16:17-18). Once you armed with this understanding and submitted under the leadership of the Holy Spirit, you will know when and where to execute authority.

Be Loyal To The Authority Over You

It is absolutely impossible to be stubborn to the authority over you and yet expect to walk in authority. It is a spiritual principle that is very vital in leadership. Anyone trying to walk effectively in authority (even having authority over those subjected to him) must also himself be subject to the authority over him. This authority could be represented by things like the Word of God, God's divine mandate, or spiritual mentorship. Take note that Jesus was also under authority as He would say of Himself: "Verily, verily, I say on to you, what he seeth the father do: for what things so ever he doeth, these also doeth the son likewise (John 5:19)." He also told us in John 15:5, "I am the vine; ye are the branches…for without Me ye can do nothing."

It is also interesting to know that God the Father Himself is under authority – The authority of His Word. It is written of Him: "for Thou hast magnified Thy Word above all Thy Name (Psalm 138:2)." This actually implies that He is not permitted to do anything except that which His word has declared. And out of His word, He is powerless. No doubt He says in Isaiah 55:11: … "So shall My word be that goeth forth out of My mouth: it shall not return unto Me void, but it shall accomplish that which I please, and it shall prosper in the thing whereto I sent it." In fact, effective leadership is only as effective to the extent to which the leader submits to the leadership over his life. The only person who does not need a leader is a dealer.

Give Instructions and Stick to Them—Not Opinions or Suggestions

This is a very vital principle in having and maintaining your position and authority over the people you lead. This of course is not trying to be a dictator, where no one should dare question the validity of your decisions. No! It is always important to give room for the leadership within your organization to inquire of you about certain decisions you make. This way they may also feel involved and not as though you are simply trying to Lord it over them. This is actually incorporation leadership. But 90% of the time, you should examine situations and circumstances properly before taking a decision. Once the decision has been taken, you are no longer in need of the opinion of those you are leading. Therefore, you should not pass it to your subordinates as though it's a suggestion. Let it rather carry the tone of an instruction which they have to comply to. When Jesus in the text told the disciple to follow Him, it wasn't a suggestion but an instruction.

So irrespective of the challenges, stick to the instructions and the people will in turn comply. Otherwise, once you are noted for not sticking to your decisions, neither you nor your instructions will be taken seriously. People will find it hard to dedicate themselves completely to such leadership. They behave that way not because they are simply being rebellious, but because they do not trust the leadership. This, friends, is a very destructive state of leadership and ministry to reach.

Be Fully Convicted Of The Feasibility of Your Decision

People want to see in your eyes a firm conviction that what you have decided is feasible and is the right thing to do. Once you have a good record in this domain of your leadership (i.e. your convictions and decisions yielding expected results), they will take your decisions seriously. If this be the case, your authority over them will always be guaranteed.

You Are The Leader! Never Create The Impression That "We" Are Leading

I am reminded of the famous quote: "A ship can only have one captain". I do not know how true the proverb is since I am not a sailor. But the proverb, whether true or false, will apply to every institution. There can never be two CEOs or two general managers no matter how big a company is. Notice that the final decision must flow from the head of the Organization. No matter how close your relationship is to your collaborators, they must realize that you are the head and that the final decision comes from no other individual but you. If not, they will soon start competing with you as opposed to being loyal. It must be made clear that, although they are in charge of certain departments within the ministry or organization, you are the one leading and they are followers. Anyone who finds this fact a bitter pill to swallow must be dismissed immediately from the administration of the organization. Such a person is a bad tree which must be cut before it starts bearing fruits. Scripture is quite clear on this when it says in Luke 3:9: "And now also the axe is laid unto the root of the tree: every tree therefore which bringeth not forth good fruit is hewn down, and cast into the fire." The administration of every organization will only succeed as long as it has followers who are collaborative, submissive, and loyal to the main leadership.

Have The Courage To Stand By Your Convictions

Looking at the main text, Jesus told Simon and Andrew with all boldness and assurance to "follow Him and He will make them fishers of men (Mark 1:1)". He was both confident and specific in what He told them. They saw this degree of assurance from the way He spoke and consequently developed enough faith to trust His word. They quickly responded to His command, abandoning their boat and profession without fear. They trusted Him easily because they heard His sound preaching. His words alone gave them a great catch of fish (Luke 5:1-11). People want proof of your competence in leadership before they follow you. They have no problem abandoning certain things, as long as you prove to them that their present and future are more glorious under your leadership.

Prove To The People That You Have Their Best Interests At Heart

Before people decide to follow a vision and be totally loyal to a man's authority, they would want to know how such a leadership and mentorship will benefit their own lives, whether spiritually, socially, physically, or otherwise. This is not greed on their part, but a desire for fulfilment and relevance. Just as Jesus had said ... "Come ye after Me and I will make you to become fishers of men (Matthew 4:19)". Unfortunately, many leaders have failed to minister to people in all spheres of their lives (spiritually, socially, and physically). This defines unproductive leadership.

Jesus, as a child, grew under the leadership of His parents. This is stated in Luke 2:51-52: "And he went down with them, and came to Nazareth, and was subject unto them... And Jesus increased in wisdom (mental growth), and stature (physical growth), and in favour with God (spiritual growth) and in favor with man (social growth)." This scripture implies that He was brought up under balanced and matured leadership. This was no doubt a contributing factor to the effectiveness of His ministry and His ability to minister to the people holistically, to the point that He hit His mark in ministry within three and a half years. The level of balance and maturity in leadership determines its fruitfulness in birthing better generations of leaders and ministries.

Chapter Eight

THE LEADER'S REFLEX ACTION

$\mathcal{I}$n this chapter, we treat a series of spontaneous and simultaneous actions a leader would immediately take in order to respond to or address certain unforeseen happenings.

The Implications of Leadership

It must be noted that leadership is the bedrock on which success as well as failure rises and falls. This would therefore imply that leadership must receive serious attention. All those engaging in leadership, despite the level, must realize that the lives of people, institutions, etc. will depend on them, and that they will be held accountable for the manner in which they lead. Having this in mind, leadership should not be seen as an opportunity for fame but as the immediate determining factor for success. All leaders have to come to a point where they no longer live for themselves, but for their mandates. It is with this consciousness that Apostle Paul said, "We do not fight as one beating the air (1 Corinthians 9:26)."

The Reflex

Due to the demands that every mandate has upon the leader as well as ministry, there are situations that will need the leader to spontaneously react. This must not be done irrationally; else more complexities may be the outcome. When situations necessitate a spontaneous reaction by the leader, the use of bureaucracy may become more of a hindrance than a help. This would mean an effective leader must be one who knows how to react spontaneously as the situation demands. Such a leader must be able to provide an appropriate solution, .i.e. a kind of reflex action. This does not, however, mean that a leader should panic and be impatient in the face of crisis. Consider the leadership attributes of Jesus Christ in the texts below:

> Now when He came to His disciples, He saw a great multitude around them, and scribes disputing with them. Then immediately all the people, when they saw Him, were greatly amazed, and began running to Him to greet Him. He then asked the scribes, "What are you disputing about?" Now one of the multitudes answered and said, "Teacher, I brought to you my son who has a mute spirit… And I spoke to your disciples that they should cast him out, and they could not" He answered him, and said, "O faithless generation, how long will I be with you? How long will I bear with you? Bring him to Me." So they brought him to Him. And when he saw Him immediately the spirit convulsed him. And he fell on the ground and wallowed, foaming at the mouth…. When Jesus saw that the people came running together, He rebuked the unclean spirit, saying to him, "You deaf and mute spirit, I command you, come out of him and enter no more into him". Then the spirit cried, and greatly convulsed him and came out of him…Now when He came into the house, His disciples asked him privately, "why could we not cast it out?" Then He said to them, "This kind can come out by nothing but prayer (and fasting)". Now they departed from there and passed through Galilee. And He did not want anyone to know about it. For He taught His disciples… Mark 9:14-31.

The above text as well as many other scriptural texts in the Bible portray the fact that every time Jesus found a deficiency in the lives of His disciples, He took them to a quiet place, far from every distraction, and spent time teaching them and imparting wisdom. This action of Jesus was always spontaneous. He would not waste time nor allow them another minute in their ignorance or shortcoming. He also rebuked the Pharisees (Matthew 23) for their errors with respect to God's Word and temple service and then He departed from the temple (Matthew 24:1-4). But His disciples did not see why He had to rebuke the Pharisees. They instead tried to call His attention to the great temple building. As such, Jesus took them to a quiet place to teach them and the first thing which He addressed was the fact that they should not be deceived and be impressed by the magnificent building. He made all things clear to them so that their faith does not stand on things that have no eternal value.

His response to such deficiencies was always quick. This made the disciples strong in faith and intolerant of contrary opinions. For this reason, in their various epistles, they kept warning the brethren on the need to defend the faith from error. This quick response of putting things in order is a very vital leadership quality. Unfortunately, this quality seems to be missing from modern-day church leaders. Many have failed to respond quickly to contrary doctrines, resulting in the flock of God wandering and finding themselves in unfavourable situations. The presence of the shepherds (leaders) has not prevented the sheep from scattering because the shepherds are not doing what they ought to do. This has put the church in a very critical position.

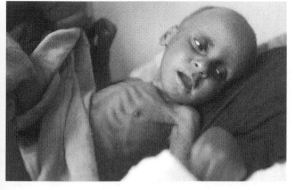

Looking at this picture, one can easily say that the state of the church today is comparable to the state of this malnourished child who is at the point of death. If anything must be done to save his life, it must be done now and effectively. The more that time is wasted in responding to the needs of this child, the more the child is exposed to the cold pangs of death. This presents us with a leadership challenge that involves quickly identifying issues within people that are not supposed to be there. When faced with issues of a critical nature, quick, spontaneous responses are what is needed to effect the appropriate change and likely redeem the situation. When one looks at the attitudes Jesus entrenched into His disciples and apostles, one would see how spontaneous they were in reacting to many critical issues. The life and ministry of Jude is a perfect illustration of this point. When he wanted to write about issues concerning salvation but realized that a lot of false teachings had become the order of the day, he immediately changed his mind to address the issue: "Beloved, when I gave all diligence to write unto you of the common salvation, it was needful for me to write unto you, and exhort you that ye should earnestly contend for the faith which was once delivered unto the saints (Jude 3)."

The Greek word for "diligence" is "spoude", which is translated "with haste" or "earnestness". The word comes from the Greek word "spendo" which means "to speed", or "to hasten". Therefore, whatever concerns service to the Lord must be made a priority and treated as a matter of urgency. How much value we place on the things of the Lord is demonstrated by our level of devotion. Challenges faced are often at the primary stage, which can easily be handled before it evolves to the secondary and tertiary stages, which are more complicated and difficult to overcome. Therefore, every leader must be smart and sensitive to identify and address issues in the lives of people quickly, before it grows uncontrollably.

Get Rid Of The Dogmatic Mindset

One reason that leaders fail to respond spontaneously to issues that deserve attention is because of a dogmatic or religious mindset. This type of mindset is one that is not flexible, and has been conditioned to do things in a particular way and in a particular order. This was the case of both the priest and Levite who failed to attend to the man who was overtaken by thieves and was left half-dead on the Jerusalem-Jericho highway. They were probably in a hurry to get to some temple service and yet failed to realize the true essence of the Gospel—which is love towards one another and ministering to those in need. Jesus refused to commend them because they failed to minister to the dying man. Such stories were written for our instruction and yet we often fail to heed the lessons, committing the same errors as a result. Many church leaders have not considered the needy in our assemblies to minister to them; rather, they have pronounced blessings upon them from a distance. This is absolutely wrong and the Bible reprimands such attitudes.

In Mark 9:14-31, Jesus was astonished by the faithlessness of his disciples when He realized that they could not cast out the spirit from the boy, and he said "…how long will I be with you? How long will I bear with you? (NKJV)" Dearly beloved, as this study comes to a close, I would like to draw your attention to the fact that God watches over His leaders, with eagerness, to celebrate the results of their effectiveness. Jesus said of unproductive leaders in John 15:2: "Every branch in me that beareth not fruit He taketh away: and every branch that beareth fruit, he purgeth it, that it may bring forth more fruit". Jesus was troubled about the fact that His disciples could not cast out the spirit considering that He was with them for about three and a half years! To Him, it was enough a time for a young convert to grow into maturity and effectiveness in leadership without any excuse for failure.

Today, unfortunately, three and a half years in the faith still counts as a good excuse for immaturity. I wish to encourage and challenge every leader to ensure that by the time a convert is in church for this amount of time, he or she should have grown into full maturity. By this time, they should be an effective leader who is pursuing and executing the purposes of God. For this to be possible, we must dedicate ourselves and our time to render effective ministry to the people— and with haste just as Christ did. It is now time for us to begin to consummate all that which we've learned, for that is the beauty of this book and what gives God glory. See you at the fore-front of life's battles as you carry the people of God to the next level of glory for their lives!

*All scriptures are taken from the King James Version of the Bible unless otherwise noted.

About the Author

Willibroad W. Ticha (PhD) is founder and president of Gospel Heroes World Missions (an international apostolic movement). He also heads Gospel Heroes Commission International, a mentorship program for ministers. His passion and engagement for the advancement of the Great Commission has caused him to address councils of bishops and pastors in several nations. He hosts revival leadership conferences across the globe, focusing on building an army for the salvation of souls. He is also a lecturer on missions and leadership affairs in various Christian universities. He is bold and extremely daring in the execution of his ministry assignments, wholeheartedly subscribing to the sentiments of George W. Bush when he said, "The risk of comfortable inaction is more risky than the risk of action."

For more information on this and other enriching books By Dr. Willibroad W. Ticha, please contact us at gospelheroes18@gmail.com!

Other book titles include:

Reclaiming Yourself from Emotional Trauma
The Battle of the Eye
Recovering Your Anointing
The Esau Syndrome
Understanding and Interpreting Dreams and Visions

Made in the USA
Lexington, KY
27 November 2019

57783625R00041